FORECASTING

for Control and Profit

FORECASTING

for Control and Profit

DAVID A. BOWERS, PH.D.

CRISP PUBLICATIONS

Editor-in-Chief: *William F. Christopher*

Managing Editor: *Kathleen Barcos*

Editor: *Evan Stubblefield*

Cover Design: *Kathleen Barcos*

Cover Production: *Russell Leong Design*

Book Design & Production: *London Road Design*

Printer: *Bawden Printing*

Library of Congress Card Catalog Number 97-65797

ISBN 1-56052-433-2

CONTENTS

I.

INTRODUCTION AND OVERVIEW

A S INDICATED BY THE TITLE, this book is about forecasting—trying to foretell the future. I have been told that on the books of New York state there is an old law, originally directed at Gypsy fortune tellers, making it a crime to claim the ability to foresee the future. Fortunately, it has never been applied to Wall Street. Hopefully, it will never be applied to me.

Actually, most of us have no choice but to try to predict the future. To live is to plan; to plan is to forecast. Forecasting is not so much a proud science as it is a necessary part of planning our future. Serious forecasting is part of the scientific method. One weighs the evidence, decides what is most likely to happen and proclaims that to be the forecast on which plans for the future will be based. This applies to planning a vacation as well as scheduling a factory's production. You don't plan a ski trip in July because snow is not in the forecast. You don't schedule a factory to produce goods you can't sell.

Of course, the more precise one's forecast, the more likely it is to be wrong. It is a lot safer to say "up" than it is to say "up to 5,406.2 by Tuesday at 10:00 A.M." Most precise numerical forecasts are sure to be wrong. It is only a matter of in which direction and by how much.

There is much in this world that cannot be forecast. Hence, the old cliché "it is better to be lucky that smart." It is not a wise strategy to plan on being lucky. It is all right to bet on the long-shot at the race track for fun, or on the underdog in an athletic event, but that is with money you can afford to lose. We are concerned here with forecasting for serious decision-making purposes. Our attitude towards the company controller who bets the company cash at the race track and wins—is to claim all the money for the company and fire the controller! He was not smart, just lucky!

How do you make and evaluate a forecast? There are scores of books and hundreds of technical papers on the subject. In this book we are restricting ourselves to what you can do with a pencil, an eraser, a pad of paper and a hand-held calculator. We are only going to explore forecasting methods that are intuitively obvious, or at least those that can be made to seem so after we have looked at them.

As noted above, our approach is to use all the available information to determine the most likely outcome and declare it to be our forecast. We will then see that what is "most likely" is almost never exactly what happens. Sometimes it is not even close. But each mistake is a lesson. Each error is a piece of information to be used in improving our forecasting techniques.

Using Error Terms

An *error term* is the difference between our forecast and what actually happens. Numerically, we subtract the actual from the forecast so if our forecast is high, we get a positive number. If our forecast is too low, the error term is a negative number. We forecast 25 and the world gives us 20, our error is +5. Had we forecast 15 and the actual number was 20, the error term would have been –5.

Generally, when we are selecting a forecasting technique, we apply it to history to see how well it would have worked in the past. If we get only zero error terms, the forecasting system is perfect. More likely we'll get a set of positive numbers (forecast too high), a set of negative numbers (forecast too low) or a mixture of positive and negative numbers.

If all the error terms were positive, we would say the forecasting system has an *upward bias*. If we found our forecasting systems had an upward bias, we would probably want to change the system to automatically lower future forecasts. On the other hand, if all the error terms were negative, we would conclude that the forecasting system had a *downward bias*. In this case we probably would adjust the system to raise the level of future forecasts.

We evaluate a forecasting system by the size and direction of the error terms it generates. To combine a number of error terms, we typically add them all up and divide the result by the total number of terms to get the average. However, by adding up the error terms, positive and negative error terms cancel each other out. Suppose you ran two tests of a forecasting system. For one month this system gave a forecast 5 units too high. For the next month it gave a forecast 5 units too low. On average, I would then have a zero error. But that doesn't mean I have found the perfect forecasting system. Hardly. The two error terms could also be +5,000 and –5,000 and, on average, we might still have a zero error term. A zero average error term simply means that the error terms sum to zero and the forecasts are *unbiased*. Unbiased means that, on average, the forecasts are neither predominantly too high nor too low.

In choosing a forecasting system, we want not only an unbiased forecast, but one with the smallest possible errors regardless of whether they are positive or negative. To measure this we add up our error terms without regard to sign. This gives us the *sum of absolute errors*. The average we get when we divide by the number of terms is the *average absolute error*. *Absolute* just means you ignore whether numbers are positive or negative. The same thing can be accomplished by changing all the negatives to positives.

Professional statisticians, for reasons we need not be concerned about, prefer to multiply each error by itself (which makes all the negative numbers positive). Once they have added them they get the *sum of the squared error terms*. To obtain a measure of the typical error term they have to not only divide by the number of terms, but they also have to take the square root of the result. This gives them something called the *standard error of the estimate* as a measure of how bad a particular forecasting procedure is.

In this book we make our judgments based on the sum of the absolute errors and the average absolute error. The smaller the better.

Naive Forecasts, Frequently the Best

At the outset we want to consider a class of forecasting techniques referred to as *naive forecasts*. These techniques have been given that name because they are based on the rather naive, but frequently useful assumption that tomorrow will be just like today or next year will be just like this year. In making a specific, numerical forecast, "more of the same" can refer to either the level of the number you are trying to forecast or to its rate of change. And the rate of change can refer to either the plain numerical change or to the percentage change.

For example, if this month's sales were up by $10,000 to a level of $100,000, we could forecast that sales next month would stay at the new $100,000 level. We could also reasonably forecast another increase of $10,000, making our forecast total $110,000. Or we could note that the $10,000 increase was an 11% increase over the previous month's level of $90,000 and forecast $111,000. All three forecasts ($100,000; $110,000; and $111,000) would be classed as naive forecasts since each involved nothing more than assuming "more of the same." Of course, "more of the same" was interpreted respectively as: a constant level of sales, a constant numerical change in sales and a constant percentage change in sales.

Naive forecasting techniques are among the oldest of forecasting techniques. In many ways they are just what the name implies, but they have been shown to be of substantial value. One of their major values is as a benchmark against which more complicated techniques can be measured. This author knows of many cases where these relatively simple forecasting techniques have been shown to be superior to very complex mathematical forecasting models. Unless there is an obvious improvement to be gained from using a more complicated model, the naive model is to be preferred. There are theoretical and practical reasons why "simpler is better." The major practical reasons are that naive models require neither complex calculations nor the services of highly trained statisticians.

It is frequently the case that when outside consultants or inside geniuses announce a new breakthrough in forecasting, you can deflate their discoveries by pointing out that they have either (1) rediscovered a naive model, or (2) used a more complex model when the appropriate naive model would have done as well or better. A necessary step in evaluating any forecasting technique is to compare it to whichever naive model seems most appropriate. You will find us doing that throughout this book.

II.

TIME SERIES ANALYSIS AND SEASONAL PATTERNS

A *TIME SERIES* IS A SET of data points such as a single factory's annual production, the nation's monthly housing starts, weekly sales for a shopping center, or one's daily beer consumption. It is a set of numbers that gives the level of some activity for a given period. As an aid in analyzing time series, we can generally think of them as being made up of four components: seasonal movements, trend movements, cyclical movements and random movements.

Seasonal movements are movements that are repeated over a particular time period. They may repeat annually, monthly or weekly. The rise in toy sales in December is a seasonal movement. Seasonal movements need not, however, repeat only once a year. Each month bank transactions rise dramatically at month-end. Airport traffic has a weekly pattern: high on Friday afternoons and low on Saturday mornings.

Trend movements are a continuous up (or down) movement through time. To have a trend, a time series should be to some extent forecastable simply on the basis of the passage of time. For example, the U.S. population has grown at various rates over the past 200 years, but it has grown each year. It obviously has a positive trend. A forecast of "up" would always be better than a forecast of "down." Most economic time series have a positive trend as a result of population growth. If it is a dollar denominated time series, such as personal income, inflation as well as population growth assures us of a positive trend.

Cyclical movements are those movements that make the difference between "good times" and "bad times." For many businesses this component is highly correlated with the movements in the level of general economic activity. Such businesses are very interested in whether the economy is in a recession or a boom. But there are sectors of the economy that appear to have their own private, very individual, cyclical movements.

Random movements are fluctuations in a time series that we cannot explain as seasonal, trend or cyclical. Whatever movement is left after we have done all the explaining we can do, we call random movement. Time series with a large random component, such as day-to-day stock prices, are by definition impossible to predict.

Using Seasonal Patterns to Forecast

So you have a monthly number you would like to forecast. Where do you start? With the past. Obtain as much history as possible. Ten year's data would be nice. Table 1 shows monthly housing starts in the United States from January 1986 through December 1995. In its raw form, this data doesn't tell you much. However, Tables 2 and 3, which show month-to-month changes in housing starts, reveal some interesting patterns. Note that in Tables 2 and 3 November and December have consistently negative numbers. Bad weather in much of the nation discourages construction. On the other hand, as spring weather arrives in March, there is a consistent, large increase from February.

One could take a giant step towards forecasting this time series by using seasonal patterns. But to forecast is to quantify. To quantify this seasonal pattern we ask: What's typical? Typical can be quantified by taking an average value—either in absolute or percentage terms. For example, as shown in the last column of Tables 2 and 3, December is typically 12.9 thousand units below November. In percentage terms, that is an average drop of 12.8%. March, at the other extreme, typically experiences an increase over February of 31.6 thousand units or 36.6%.

Month-to-Month Forecasting Using Seasonal Patterns

To use seasonal patterns in forecasting, we take where we are and add the typical seasonal change. What is "typical?" We can use the average columns in Tables 1, 2 and 3 to give us the typical behavior for each month.

To make a forecast one month in advance one need only add or subtract the expected seasonal movement. March 1995, for example, would be forecast to equal February 1995, 81.6 thousand, plus 31.6 thousand. The forecast would be 113.2 thousand. (The actual was 103.8

	1986	1987	1988	1989	1990	1991	1992	1993	1994	1995	Monthly Averages
January	115.6	105.1	78.2	100.1	99.2	52.5	71.6	70.5	76.2	84.5	85.4
February	107.2	102.8	90.2	85.8	86.9	59.1	78.8	74.6	83.5	81.6	85.1
March	151.0	141.2	128.8	117.8	108.5	73.8	111.6	95.5	134.3	103.8	116.6
April	188.2	159.3	153.2	129.4	119.0	99.7	107.6	117.8	137.6	116.9	132.9
May	186.6	158.0	140.2	131.7	121.1	97.7	115.2	120.9	148.8	130.5	135.1
June	183.6	162.9	150.2	143.2	117.8	103.4	117.8	128.5	136.4	123.4	136.7
July	172.0	152.4	137.0	134.7	111.2	103.5	106.2	115.3	127.8	129.1	128.9
August	163.8	143.6	136.8	122.4	102.8	94.7	109.9	121.8	139.8	135.8	127.1
September	154.0	152.0	131.1	109.3	93.1	86.5	106.0	118.5	130.1	122.4	120.3
October	154.8	139.1	135.1	130.1	94.2	101.8	111.8	123.2	130.6	126.2	124.7
November	115.6	118.8	113.0	96.6	81.4	75.6	84.5	102.3	113.4	107.2	100.8
December	113.0	85.4	94.2	95.0	57.4	65.6	78.6	98.7	98.5	92.8	87.9
Total	1805.4	1620.6	1488.0	1396.1	1192.6	1013.9	1199.6	1287.6	1457.0	1354.2	1381.5

Table 1. Total U.S. housing starts (in 1,000s)

	1986	1987	1988	1989	1990	1991	1992	1993	1994	1995	Average
January		-7.9	-7.2	5.9	4.2	-4.9	6.0	-8.1	-22.5	-14.0	-5.4
February	-8.4	-2.3	12.0	-14.3	-12.3	6.6	7.2	4.1	7.3	-2.9	-0.3
March	43.8	38.4	38.6	32.0	21.6	14.7	32.8	20.9	50.8	22.2	31.6
April	37.2	18.1	24.4	11.6	10.5	25.9	-4.0	22.3	3.3	13.1	16.2
May	-1.6	-1.3	-13.0	2.3	2.1	-2.0	7.6	3.1	11.2	13.6	2.2
June	-3.0	4.9	10.0	11.5	-3.3	5.7	2.6	7.6	-12.4	-7.1	1.7
July	-11.6	-10.5	-13.2	-8.5	-6.6	0.1	-11.6	-13.2	-8.6	5.7	-7.8
August	-8.2	-8.8	-0.2	-12.3	-8.4	-8.8	3.7	6.5	12.0	6.7	-1.8
September	-9.8	8.4	-5.7	-13.1	-9.7	-8.2	-3.9	-3.3	-9.7	-13.4	-6.8
October	0.8	-12.9	4.0	20.8	1.1	15.3	5.8	4.7	0.5	3.8	4.4
November	-39.2	-20.3	-22.1	-33.5	-12.8	-26.2	-27.3	-20.9	-17.2	-19.0	-23.9
December	-2.6	-33.4	-18.8	-1.6	-24.0	-10.0	-5.9	-3.6	-14.9	-14.4	-12.9

Table 2.   Month-to-month change in total U.S. housing starts (in 1,000s)

	1986	1987	1988	1989	1990	1991	1992	1993	1994	1995	Average
January	−7.3	−7.0	−8.4	6.3	4.4	−8.5	9.1	−10.3	−22.8	−14.2	−5.7
February	40.9	−2.2	15.3	−14.3	−12.4	12.6	10.1	5.8	9.6	−3.4	1.4
March	24.6	37.4	42.8	37.3	24.9	24.9	41.6	28.0	60.8	27.2	36.6
April	−0.9	12.8	18.9	9.8	9.7	35.1	−3.6	23.4	2.5	12.6	14.6
May	−1.6	−0.8	−8.5	1.8	1.8	−2.0	7.1	2.6	8.1	11.6	2.1
June	−6.3	3.1	7.1	8.7	−2.7	5.8	2.3	6.3	−8.3	−5.4	1.5
July	−4.8	−6.4	−8.8	−5.9	−5.6	0.1	−9.8	−10.3	−6.3	4.6	−5.5
August	−6.0	−5.8	−0.1	−9.1	−7.6	−8.5	3.5	5.6	9.4	5.2	−1.2
September	0.5	5.8	−4.2	−10.7	−9.4	−8.7	−3.5	−2.7	−6.9	−9.9	−5.6
October	−25.3	−8.5	3.1	19.0	1.2	17.7	5.5	4.0	0.4	3.1	4.6
November	−2.2	−14.6	−16.4	−25.7	−13.6	−25.7	−24.4	−17.0	−13.2	−15.1	−19.1
December		−28.1	−16.6	−1.7	−29.5	−13.2	−7.0	−3.5	−13.1	−13.4	−12.8

Table 3.   Percentage change month-to-month in total U.S. housing starts

thousand.) Using percentage changes in this case (and in most cases) gives slightly better results. One merely increases February's 81.6 thousand by 36.6% to be 111.5 thousand as the forecast for March.

To illustrate:

_____	**x**	_____	**=**	_____
(This month)		(1 + % Seasonal)		(Next month)

For March 1995:

_____	**x**	_____	**=**	_____
81.6		1.366		111.5
(February 1995)		(1 + March %)		(March forecast)

Strictly speaking, we should have only used data through 1994 to calculate the seasonals we are using to forecast 1995 with. If we know 1995 figures, we don't have to forecast them. More on that later.

Dividing an Annual Forecast by Months

Let's suppose the managers at corporate headquarters have forecast (and the company has based its budget on) a 13% increase in 1994 sales over 1993. For illustrative purposes we can assume U.S. housing starts are unit sales of the XYZ Manufacturing Company. This 13% increase from a 1993 level of 1,287.6 gives us a forecast level of 1,457.0 for 1994, the actual totals shown in Table 1.

For annual budget planning +13% is fine, but suppose you have to schedule monthly manufacturing (or delivery to stores, etc.). You would need to forecast for January, February and each month thereafter. You would want to know what proportion of a total year's sales are typically accounted for each month. To determine this, add the monthly averages—in our case 1,381.5 as shown on Table 1—and take each monthly average as a percentage of the total. The results are shown in Table 4. In the first column of Table 4, the 6.2% for January is calculated by taking January's average of 85.4 from Table 1 as a percentage of the total of all monthly averages, 1,381.5. The 90.3 forecast for January 1994 is 6.2% of the expected annual total of 1,457.0.

To illustrate:

(% of Annual)	X	(Annual total)	=	(Forecast)

For January 1994:

.062	X	1,4570	=	90.3
(% for January)		(1994 total)		(January 1994)

How good is this forecast? Relative to what? A reasonable alternative might have been simply to divide up the expected annual total into twelve equal parts of 121.4 each. On the right-hand side of Table 4 we show the forecast and error terms that would result from ignoring the seasonals. The average error is 19.0 if you ignore the seasonals, but is only 6.5 using the seasonals. While 1994 did not follow the seasonal pattern exactly, the seasonal movements obviously would be useful in month-to-month scheduling.

% of Annual Total		Using Seasonal Pattern			Ignoring Seasonal Pattern	
		Fcst.	Actual	Error	Fcst.	Error
January	6.2	90.3	76.2	14.1	121.4	45.2
February	6.2	90.3	83.5	6.8	121.4	37.9
March	8.4	122.4	134.3	-11.9	121.4	-12.9
April	9.6	139.9	137.6	2.3	121.4	-16.2
May	9.8	142.8	148.8	-6.0	121.4	-15.0
June	9.9	144.2	136.4	7.8	121.4	-15.0
July	9.3	135.5	127.8	7.7	121.4	-6.4
August	9.2	134.0	139.8	-5.8	121.4	-18.4
September	8.7	126.8	130.1	-3.3	121.4	-8.7
October	9.0	131.1	130.6	0.5	121.4	-9.2
November	7.3	106.4	113.4	-7.0	121.4	8.0
December	6.4	93.2	98.5	-5.3	121.4	22.9
Total	100.0	1456.9	1457.0	-0.1	1456.8	-0.2
Sum of absolute errors				78.5		228.0
Average absolute error				6.5		19.0

Table 4. 1994 monthly forecast when total is given for the year

Seasonally Adjusting a Time Series

Seasonal Adjustment is a different way of looking at time series movements. With seasonally adjusted data, we are comparing what *actually* happened to what we *expected* to happen simply as a result of seasonal movement. The purpose of seasonally adjusting a time series is to see how you are doing excluding seasonal variation. This can be useful in observing trend and cyclical movements.

Suppose you sell toys. From November to December you expect, on the basis of seasonal movement, that sales will be up by $100,000. But sales only rise by $90,000. On a "seasonally adjusted basis" sales were *down* by $10,000. Had the increase been greater than the seasonal, perhaps up by $110,000, sales would have been *up* by $10,000 on a seasonally adjusted basis.

A *seasonally adjusted time series* is one that has had the seasonal movements taken out. It the actual movement exactly meets the expected seasonal movement, the seasonally adjusted numbers show no change. So to seasonally adjust data you reverse the seasonal movement. For example, suppose a toy store sold $100,000 in November and $200,000 in December, exactly what we expected due to seasonal movement. We would seasonally adjust December by subtracting the expected 100% increase, making December equal to November at $100,000. Apparently there is no trend or cyclical movement present.

Let's seasonally adjust the ten years of monthly data we have in Table 1. To do this we first calculate a *seasonal index,* which is the percentage a particular month represents of the overall average for all data. In this case the

overall average monthly figure for the ten years of data
(the average of the monthly averages) is 115.1. One way
to calculate this is to sum up monthly averages, as we
have done in the last column of Table 1 and in the first
column of Table 5, and divide the total by 12. In this case
we get 1381.5/12 = 115.1. January's seasonal index is the
ratio of the January average, 85.4, to the overall average,
115.1, which is .741.

The other seasonal indexes are as shown in Table 5.
One way to look at this seasonal index is that January
typically is 74.1% as big as the overall average. As we can
see from the right-hand column of Table 5, June has the
largest seasonal index at 118.8% of the average.

We should stop to note here that it is customary to
quote seasonal indexes as percentages without the percent
sign. In other words, the January index would be referred
to as 74.1 and the June index would be referred to as
118.7. But one must be respectful of the decimal point
when seasonally adjusting data.

Smoothing Seasonal Fluctuations

As indicated above, the purpose of seasonally adjusting
data is to *remove* the seasonal fluctuations, to smooth out
the data. We want to lower the months that are usually
high and raise the ones that are usually low. We do this
by *dividing* by the seasonal indexes. A month that is below
average will have an index of less than 100%, and when
we divide the raw data by it we will get a larger number.
For example, the actual figure for January 1986 was 115.6.
We increase it to 156.0 when we divide by the seasonal

	Averages	Indexes
January	85.4	0.741
February	85.1	0.739
March	116.6	1.013
April	132.9	1.154
May	135.1	1.173
June	136.7	1.188
July	128.9	1.120
August	127.1	1.104
September	120.3	1.045
October	124.7	1.083
November	100.8	0.876
December	87.9	0.764
Total	1381.5	12.000
Average	115.1	1.000

Table 5. Monthly averages and seasonal indexes

index of .741. On the other hand, a month that is typically above average will have an index of greater than 100% and when we divide by a number greater than 1.00, we will get a smaller number. For example, we must decrease June 1986 from 183.6 to 154.5 when we divide it by the June seasonal index of 1.188.

Table 6 presents the seasonally adjusted data for all ten years, 1986–95. Note that after adjustment every month has the same average, 115.1, which was the overall average of the unadjusted data (Table 5). Note, also, that the annual totals of the adjusted data are very close to the annual totals for the unadjusted data. If they are not, we have made a mistake. The reason the seasonal adjustment factors sum to 12.00 in Table 5 is that on average we are

	1986	1987	1988	1989	1990	1991	1992	1993	1994	1995	Average
January	156.0	141.8	105.5	135.0	133.8	70.8	96.6	95.1	102.8	114.0	115.1
February	145.1	139.2	122.1	116.1	117.6	80.0	106.7	101.0	113.0	110.5	115.1
March	149.1	139.4	127.1	116.3	107.1	72.8	110.2	94.3	132.6	102.5	115.1
April	163.1	138.0	132.7	112.1	103.1	86.4	93.2	102.1	119.2	101.3	115.1
May	159.0	134.7	119.5	112.3	103.2	83.3	98.2	103.0	126.8	111.2	115.1
June	154.5	137.2	126.5	120.6	99.2	87.1	99.2	108.2	114.9	103.9	115.1
July	153.6	136.1	122.3	120.3	99.3	92.4	94.8	103.0	114.1	115.3	115.1
August	148.3	130.0	123.9	110.8	93.1	85.8	99.5	110.3	126.6	123.0	115.1
September	147.4	145.5	125.5	104.6	89.1	82.8	101.4	113.4	124.5	117.1	115.1
October	142.9	128.4	124.7	120.1	87.0	94.0	103.2	113.7	120.6	116.5	115.1
November	132.0	135.6	129.0	110.3	92.9	86.3	96.5	116.8	129.5	122.4	115.1
December	148.0	111.8	123.3	124.4	75.2	85.9	102.9	129.2	129.0	121.5	115.1
Total	1799.0	1617.6	1482.2	1402.9	1200.6	1007.5	1202.4	1290.1	1453.5	1359.1	1381.5

Table 6. Total U.S. housing starts seasonally adjusted (in 1,000s)

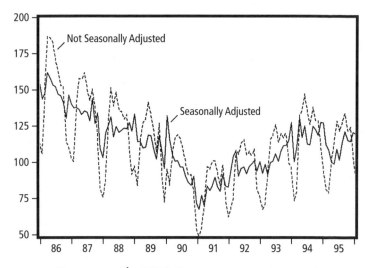

Figure 1. *Total U.S. housing starts, 1986–1995 (monthly figures in 1,000s)*

dividing each month in a year by 1.00. We are raising some and lowering others, but not changing the total for the year significantly.

The smoothing effect of seasonal adjustment is obvious from Figure 1, which shows the unadjusted and adjusted data graphically. From Figure 1 it would appear that over this time period this time series had no particular trend. It does appear to have something of a cycle, however; going from a peak in mid-1986 to a low at the end of 1990 when it began to rise again.

We will return to this series to analyze its cyclical movements after we consider a series that has a definite trend, annual data for the U.S. population.

III.

TREND ANALYSIS

A S DEFINED ABOVE, trend movements are persistent long-term growth or decline in a time series. We noted that to have a trend a time series should be to some extent forecastable on the basis of time alone. For example, let us consider U.S. population for the twenty-year period, 1973–1993.

For the first half of the period, 1973–1983, Table 7 shows that on average the population grew by 2,240 thousand each year. In percentage terms the average rate of growth during this time period was 1.01% per year. As with the seasonal movements, we have the choice of using either the absolute or percentage change. And again, we get better results with the percentage change.

How do we forecast using trend analysis? Technicians call it *extrapolation*. It means you assume the average change in the past will be the average change in the future. For example, by looking at the annual percentage change in Table 7 we might well conclude that the average of 1.01% is a good basis for forecasting. After all, the actual percentage change for the years 1974–83 did not vary greatly from the average. The highest was 1.19% in 1980

		Change	
	Level	Number	%
1973	211,909		
1974	213,854	1,945	0.92
1975	215,973	2,119	0.99
1976	218,035	2,062	0.95
1977	220,239	2,204	1.01
1978	222,585	2,346	1.07
1979	225,055	2,470	1.11
1980	227,726	2,671	1.19
1981	229,966	2,240	0.98
1982	232,188	2,222	0.97
1983	234,307	2,119	0.91
Average		2,240	1.01

*Table 7. Total U.S. population, 1973–1983
(in 1,000s)*

and the lowest was .91% in 1983. Certainly assuming an annual growth of 1.01% for any given year in the future is likely to be better than assuming a negative or zero rate of change.

Trend analysis is useful both as a component of short-term, year-to-year forecasting and as the main component of long-term, such as ten-year, forecasting. Let us consider each of these in turn.

Using Trend to Make a One-Year Forecast

To forecast one year ahead on the basis of a historical trend, we simply extrapolate one year at a time. To extrapolate one year at a time, we take this year's number and increase it by the percentage trend. For example, the 1984 forecast is 1983's level of 234,307 increased by 1.01% to get a forecast of 236,674.

To illustrate:

_____	**X**	_____	**=**	_____
(This year's actual)		(1 + % Trend)		(Next year's forecast)

For forecasting 1984:

234,307	**X**	1.0101	**=**	236,674
(1983 actual)		(1 + 1.01%)		(1984 forecast)

The actual value for 1984 was 236,348, resulting in an error of 326. This is a fairly small error considering it is less than two-tenths of one percent of the actual (.14%).

Table 8 shows actual, forecast and error terms for 1984–93, using trend and ignoring trend. Each forecast was based on the actual for the previous year. This is not a ten-year forecast, but a series of one-year forecasts. In Table 8 we have also made a forecast ignoring trend on a year-to-year basis by assuming the coming year will stay at the level of the current year. Obviously, using trends improves our forecasts as it reduces our errors dramatically. Ignoring the trend the average absolute error is 2,394, while using the trend reduces the absolute error to 224, a reduction of about 90%.

Total U.S. Population (in 1,000s)					
		Using Trend		Ignoring Trend	
	Actual	**Forecast**	**Error**	**Forecast**	**Error**
1984	236,348	236,674	326	234,307	-2,041
1985	238,466	238,735	269	236,348	-2,118
1986	240,651	240,875	224	238,466	-2,185
1987	242,804	243,082	278	240,651	-2,153
1988	245,021	245,256	235	242,804	-2,217
1989	247,342	247,496	154	245,021	-2,321
1990	249,908	249,840	-68	247,342	-2,566
1991	252,648	252,432	-216	249,908	-2,740
1992	255,458	255,200	-258	252,648	-2,810
1993	258,245	258,038	-207	255,458	-2,787
Sum of absolute errors			2,235		23,938
Average absolute error			224		2,394

Table 8.   A series of one-year forecasts

Using Trend to Make a Ten-Year Forecast

To forecast ten years in advance we must extrapolate ten years. The big difference from a one-year forecast is we cannot assume to know the value of 1992 when we are forecasting for 1993. We are limited with knowing only 1983's actual value. Table 9 gives a set of forecasts out ten years beginning with 1984. We use the same procedure we used with the one-year forecast except that for every year after 1983 we have to insert a *forecast* not an *actual* number. For example, the forecast for 1985 is 101.01% of the forecast for 1984 since we do not know the actual.

To illustrate:

$$\underline{\quad\quad\quad} \times \underline{\quad\quad\quad} = \underline{\quad\quad\quad}$$

(This year's forecast)   (1 + % Trend)   (Next year's forecast)

For forecasting 1985:

$$\frac{236{,}674}{\text{(1984 forecast)}} \times \frac{1.0101}{(1 + 1.01\%)} = \frac{239{,}064}{\text{(1985 forecast)}}$$

For forecasting 1986:

$$\frac{239{,}064}{\text{(1985 forecast)}} \times \frac{1.0101}{(1 + 1.01\%)} = \frac{241{,}478}{\text{(1986 forecast)}}$$

We can continue this sequence as far out as we wish to extrapolate the trend. Table 9 shows such an extrapolation out ten years. The error terms are, of course, much larger than those used for the one-year forecasts. An eternal truth seems to be that the further ahead one tries to forecast, the less accurate one will be.

The trend is, however, making a substantial contribution to our forecasting accuracy. This can be seen from a comparison of the two error columns in Table 9. The second set of forecasts and errors on the right of Table 9 ignore the trend by assuming that the population does not grow, that it stays constant at the 1983 level (Table 7). This results in total errors (all negative) of 123,820 and an average error term of 12,382. When using the trend to extrapolate, the total errors (all positive) are 10,360 for an

Total U.S. Population (in 1,000s)					
		Using Trend		Ignoring Trend	
	Actual	**Forecast**	**Error**	**Forecast**	**Error**
1984	236,348	236,674	326	234,307	-2,041
1985	238,466	239,064	598	234,307	-4,159
1986	240,651	241,478	827	234,307	-6,344
1987	242,804	243,917	1,113	234,307	-8,497
1988	245,021	246,381	1,360	234,307	-10,714
1989	247,342	248,869	1,527	234,307	-13,035
1990	249,908	251,383	1,475	234,307	-15,601
1991	252,648	253,922	1,274	234,307	-18,341
1992	255,458	256,487	1,029	234,307	-21,151
1993	258,245	259,077	832	234,307	-23,938
Average	246,689	247,725	1,036	234,307	-12,382
Sum of absolute errors			10,360		123,820
Average absolute error			1,036		12,382

Table 9.   A ten-year forecast

average of 1,036. Again, we reduce the average absolute error by over 90% by using the trend.

IV.

CYCLICAL ANALYSIS

THE ESSENCE OF CYCLICAL ANALYSIS is predicting turning points—that point at which the general direction of movement changes from up to down, or from down to up. Cyclical turning points are referred to as *peaks* and *troughs*. Peaks indicate the change in direction from up to down. Troughs (pronounced "troffs") indicate the change in direction from down to up.

In Figure 1, both the unadjusted and seasonally adjusted housing starts show what is apparently a cyclical turning point, a trough, around December of 1990. The general direction from 1986 through 1990 was down; from the end of 1990 through 1995, the general direction was up. It would have been useful in December of 1990 to know that housing starts had indeed hit bottom and that a cyclical recovery was underway.

Figure 2 presents a longer view of this time series, showing annual data for 21 years. There is a clear cyclical pattern. Between turning points, forecasting using a rough trend analysis would probably be fairly accurate. But how can you forecast turning points?

Rates of Change and "Pressure Curves" as Cyclical Indicators

Many methods for anticipating turning points are based on the idea that a time series slows down before it turns down. A reasonable approach is that if your sales each of the last three years increased by 15, then 10, and most recently by only 2, you might feel a decrease in sales is likely the following year. Similarly, the rate at which something is falling usually slows down before it begins to peak.

Table 10 shows the numerical data for Figure 2, annual housing starts for 21 years. The second column of data on Table 10 shows the *change* in the level of housing starts from one year to the next. To the right of both columns of data in the table, a "P" indicates a peak turn-

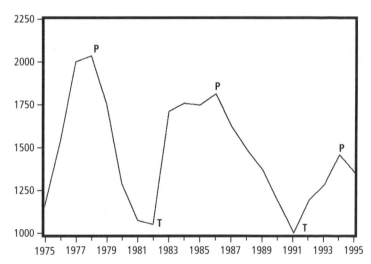

Figure 2. Total U.S. housing starts, 1975–1995 (annual data in 1,000s)

28

Year	Level	Change
1975	1160.4	
1976	1537.3	376.9
1977	1987.1	449.8 P
1978	2020.3 P	33.2
1979	1745.0	-275.3
1980	1292.2	-452.8 T
1981	1084.1	-208.1
1982	1062.2 T	-21.9
1983	1703.0	640.8 P
1984	1749.4	46.4
1985	1741.7	-7.7
1986	1805.4 P	63.7
1987	1620.6	-184.8 T
1988	1488.0	-132.6
1989	1376.1	-111.9
1990	1192.6	-183.5
1991	1013.9 T	-178.7
1992	1199.6	185.7 P
1993	1287.6	88.0
1994	1457.0 P	169.4
1995	1354.2	-102.8

Table 10.   The cyclical behavior of total U.S. housing starts (annual data, 1975–1995)

ing point and a "T" a trough. Figure 3 is a graph of the level and the year-to-year change. In the table and in Figure 3, we can see that the turning points in the rate of change occur a year or more before the turning points in the underlying data. In other words, the rate of increase begins to fall before a peak is reached, and the rate of decrease slows before a trough is reached. (This is a mathematical necessity of any relatively smooth series.)

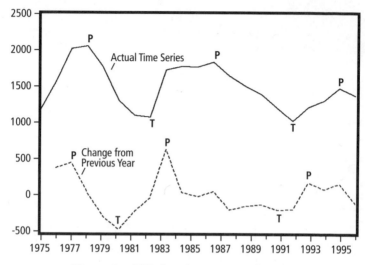

Figure 3.   U.S. housing starts, 1975–1995
(annual data in 1,000s)

Another variation on the rate of change as a leading indicator is the use of *pressure curves*. Instead of a change one year to the next, or one month to the next, pressure curves consider the rate of change over various time periods. For example, if you were working with monthly data a 1/1 pressure curve would be the ratio of this month to last month; a 3/3 pressure curve would be the ratio of the most recent three months to the previous three months; and so on. If the time series is increasing, the ratio will be greater than 1.00 and the pressure curve will be above 100, as it is again customary to speak in terms of percentages without the percent sign.

Figure 4 is a graph of annual housing starts for 21 years on a monthly basis, seasonally adjusted. Also

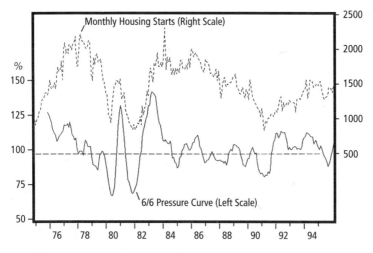

Figure 4. ***Monthly housing starts and a 6/6 pressure curve***
(annual data in 1,000s)

shown on the graph is a 6/6 pressure curve. This pressure curve is calculated by taking the ratio of the total
data for the most recent six months to the total data six
months prior to that. A pressure curve point can be calculated for each month (excluding the first twelve).

Note the pressure curve fell below 100 in early 1978,
about the time housing starts peaked. Both curves hit bottom in 1981, with the pressure curve falling below 100
again in 1984, preceding a long decline in housing starts.
When the pressure curve finally rose above 100 to stay
in mid-1991, it indicated a cyclical turn. As a generality,
when the pressure curve was below 100, the series was in
a down cycle; when the pressure curve was above 100, the
series was in a up cycle.

Choosing Pressure Curves

How do you choose what pressure curve to use with what series? You experiment by trying various combinations and lag times. We will revisit this question later.

Here, we will note that any pressure curve comparing data with the same period a year earlier can be used without seasonally adjusting the data. For example, a 1/12 curve is plotted by taking the ratio of this month to the same month a year ago, January 1995 to January 1994, etc. This very common measure is somewhat rough, but it is a good, quick check on the annual growth rate of a time series.

V.

"EXPONENTIAL SMOOTHING" IS REALLY JUST ERROR CORRECTION

W E HAD A SECTION IN Chapter I entitled "Using Error Terms." There we stated that we would choose the forecasting procedure that gave us the smallest error terms. Now we want to consider a forecasting system in which the forecast for the coming month corrects for the error we made this month. If we forecast too *low* for February, we raise the forecast for March. If we forecast too *high* for February, we lower the forecast for March.

For example, consider the actual monthly housing starts (seasonally adjusted) for five years shown in the first column of Table 11. Even after seasonal adjustment they still fluctuate quite a bit. One way to at least stay with the business cycle is to simply state next month will be the same as last month. The very first number, January 1991, is 70.8; so my forecast for February is 70.8. February turns out to be 80.0; so I adjust my forecast upward to

80.0. Adjusting all the way up to 80.0 proves to be a mistake as the March figure is only 72.8.

Maybe I shouldn't change my forecast by 100% of the error. Maybe only 80%, 50%, or 20%. A partial error adjustment forecasting system is referred to as *exponential smoothing*. The first "forecast" column in Table 11 is a 100% error correction forecast (one of our naive forecasting techniques). Actually, in this case it works well. The average absolute error shown at the bottom of the third column is 6.9, only 6.5% of the average level of 105.8.

Adjusting an Error Term

Perhaps a little less than 100% error correction would work better? The second set of forecasts in Table 11 is derived by adjusting for 80% of the previous month's error. We start with the naive forecast assuming February will be the same as January at 70.8. The result is an error term for February of –9.2. If we adjusted for 100% of the error we would add 9.2 to our old forecast of 70.8 and get 80.0. This would make our March forecast, 80.0, equal to our February actual. However, if we only want an 80% adjustment, we multiply the error term, 9.2, times .80 to get an adjustment of only 7.4. We add the 7.4 to the February forecast of 70.8 to get a March forecast of 78.2.

Correcting for only 80% of our error gives us the forecasts and error terms shown in Table 11 under .8. At the bottom of the table we see that the average absolute error over the five-year period is only 6.5. This is better than we got with 100% adjustment which gave us an average error term of 6.9. Well, if cutting our error adjustment factor from 100% to 80% improves things, why not try a lower number, such as 50%. And as shown under .5 in Table 11, the average error falls even further to 6.3. Great! Let's try an adjustment of only 20%. Whoops! At .20, the average error term jumps up to 7.2. The ideal error adjustment must be somewhere below 50% and above 20%.

This type of forecasting system has a number of advantages. First, you do not have to have a long history of data to use it—just one month's forecast and one month's actual. A second advantage is that the computations are simple, easy and straightforward. To get next month's forecast, we simply multiply the error term by the correction factor and add it to this month's forecast.

Choosing the Best
Error Correction Factor

So far we have implied that the size of the error correction factor was to be determined solely by the size of the corrected error terms. That is not the whole story. The solid line in Figure 5 shows a time series that behaves very differently in the first half of the time period than in the second half. For the first 25 data points the series bounces around the average value of 444 quite a bit. For the second 25 data points we can observe a definite upward trend with smaller fluctuations.

This is a realistic example. In many businesses a time series has been bouncing around a fixed value for years, but managers would like to be alerted if a positive or negative trend should develop. For example, a manufacturer of nuts and bolts has hundreds of individual products being

	Actual (Seas. Adj.)	Error Correction Factor							
		1.0		0.8		0.5		0.2	
		Fcst.	Error	Fcst.	Error	Fcst.	Error	Fcst.	Error
1991									
January	70.8								
February	80.0	70.8	-9.2	70.8	-9.2	70.8	-9.2	70.8	-9.2
March	72.8	80.0	7.2	78.2	5.3	75.4	2.6	72.6	-0.2
April	86.4	72.8	-13.5	73.9	-12.5	74.1	-12.3	72.7	-13.7
May	83.3	86.4	3.1	83.9	0.6	80.3	-3.0	75.4	-7.9
June	87.1	83.3	-3.8	83.4	-3.7	81.8	-5.3	77.0	-10.1
July	92.4	87.1	-5.4	86.3	-6.1	84.4	-8.0	79.0	-13.4
August	85.8	92.4	6.7	91.2	5.5	88.4	2.7	81.7	-4.1
September	82.8	85.8	3.0	86.8	4.1	87.1	4.3	82.5	-0.3
October	94.0	82.8	-11.2	83.6	-10.4	84.9	-9.1	82.6	-11.4
November	86.3	94.0	7.7	91.9	5.6	89.5	3.2	84.8	-1.5
December	85.9	86.3	0.4	87.4	1.5	87.9	2.0	85.1	-0.8
1992									
January	96.6	85.9	-10.7	88.2	-10.4	86.9	-9.7	85.3	-11.3
February	106.7	96.6	-10.1	94.5	-12.2	91.7	-14.9	87.5	-19.1
March	110.2	106.7	-3.5	104.2	-5.9	99.2	-11.0	91.4	-18.8
April	93.2	110.2	16.9	109.0	15.7	104.7	11.5	95.1	1.9
May	98.2	93.2	-5.0	96.4	-1.8	99.0	0.8	94.7	-3.4
June	99.2	98.2	-1.0	97.8	-1.4	98.6	-0.6	95.4	-3.8
July	94.8	99.2	4.4	98.9	4.1	98.9	4.0	96.2	1.4
August	99.5	94.8	-4.7	95.7	-3.9	96.9	-2.7	95.9	-3.6
September	101.4	99.5	-1.9	98.7	-2.7	98.2	-3.3	96.6	-4.8
October	103.2	101.4	-1.8	100.9	-2.3	99.8	-3.4	97.6	-5.6
November	96.5	103.2	6.8	102.8	6.3	101.5	5.0	98.7	2.3
December	102.9	96.5	-6.5	97.7	-5.2	99.0	-3.9	98.3	-4.6
1993									
January	95.1	102.9	7.8	101.9	6.8	101.0	5.9	99.2	4.1
February	101.0	95.1	-5.9	96.5	-4.5	98.0	-3.0	98.4	-2.8
March	94.3	101.0	6.7	100.1	5.8	99.5	5.2	98.9	4.6
April	102.1	94.3	-7.8	95.4	-6.6	96.9	-5.2	98.0	-4.1
May	103.0	102.1	-1.0	100.7	-2.3	99.5	-3.6	98.8	-4.3
June	108.2	103.0	-5.2	102.6	-5.6	101.3	-6.9	99.6	-8.6
July	103.0	108.2	5.2	107.1	4.1	104.7	1.8	101.4	-1.6
August	110.3	103.0	-7.3	103.8	-6.5	103.8	-6.4	101.7	-8.6
September	113.4	110.3	-3.1	109.0	-4.4	107.1	-6.3	103.4	-10.0
October	113.7	113.4	-0.3	112.5	-1.2	110.2	-3.5	105.4	-8.3
November	116.8	113.7	-3.0	113.5	-3.3	112.0	-4.8	107.1	-9.7
December	129.2	116.8	-12.4	116.1	-13.1	114.4	-14.8	109.0	-20.2

Table 11.   Forecasting monthy housing starts using an error correction model

36

	Actual (Seas. Adj.)	Error Correction Factor							
		1.0		0.8		0.5		0.2	
		Fcst.	Error	Fcst.	Error	Fcst.	Error	Fcst.	Error
1994									
January	102.8	129.2	26.5	126.6	23.8	121.8	19.0	113.1	10.3
February	113.0	102.8	-10.2	107.6	-5.5	112.3	-0.7	111.0	-2.0
March	132.6	113.0	-19.5	111.9	-20.6	112.7	-19.9	111.4	-21.2
April	119.2	132.6	13.3	128.4	9.2	122.6	3.4	115.6	-3.6
May	126.8	119.2	-7.6	121.1	-5.8	120.9	-5.9	116.4	-10.5
June	114.9	126.8	12.0	125.7	10.8	123.9	9.0	118.5	3.6
July	114.1	114.9	0.7	117.0	2.9	119.4	5.2	117.7	3.6
August	126.6	114.1	-12.5	114.7	-11.9	116.7	-9.8	117.0	-9.6
September	124.5	126.6	2.1	124.2	-0.3	121.7	-2.8	118.9	-5.6
October	120.6	124.5	3.9	124.4	3.9	123.1	2.5	120.0	-0.5
November	129.5	120.6	-8.9	121.4	-8.1	121.8	-7.6	120.1	-9.3
December	129.0	129.5	0.5	127.8	-1.1	125.6	-3.3	122.0	-7.0
1995									
January	114.0	129.0	15.0	128.8	14.8	127.3	13.3	123.4	9.4
February	110.5	114.0	3.5	118.9	6.5	120.6	10.2	121.5	11.1
March	102.5	110.5	8.0	111.8	9.3	115.6	13.1	119.3	16.8
April	101.3	102.5	1.2	104.3	3.0	109.0	7.7	115.9	14.7
May	111.2	101.3	-9.9	101.9	-9.3	105.1	-6.1	113.0	1.8
June	103.9	111.2	7.3	109.4	5.5	108.2	4.3	112.7	8.7
July	115.3	103.9	-11.4	105.0	-10.3	106.0	-9.2	110.9	-4.4
August	123.0	115.3	-7.7	113.2	-9.7	110.7	-12.3	111.8	-11.2
September	117.1	123.0	5.8	121.0	3.9	116.8	-0.3	114.0	-3.1
October	116.5	117.1	0.6	117.9	1.4	117.0	0.5	114.6	-1.9
November	122.4	116.5	-5.9	116.8	-5.6	116.7	-5.6	115.0	-7.4
December	121.5	122.4	0.9	121.3	-0.2	119.6	-1.9	116.5	-5.0
Total	6241.9	6191.2		8178.6		6142.4		6008.4	
Average	105.8	104.9		104.7		104.1		101.8	
Sum of Absolute Errors			405.0		384.0		373.7		421.9
Average Absolute Error			6.9		6.5		6.3		7.2

Table 11. Forecasting monthly housing starts using an error correction model (continued)

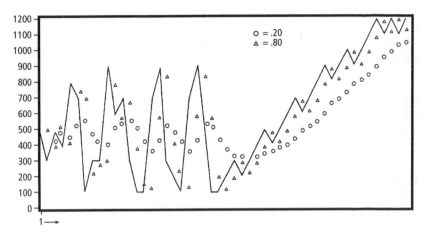

Figure 5. *Exponential smoothing forecasts based on 20% and 80% correction factors*

sold for a wide variety of uses. He schedules production on the basis of sales forecasts generated by exponential smoothing. Should he use a relatively small error correction factor, such as .20, or a relatively large one, such as .80? In Figure 5, forecasts generated using .20 are represented by 0s, while the forecasts generated by an error correction factor of .80 are represented by △s. For the first 25 periods when the time series is fluctuating around a fixed value, the accuracy of the two sets of forecasts are about the same. The average absolute error is 263 when the error correction factor is .2, and 265 when .80 is used—not significantly different.

Since both values of the error correction factor give equally inaccurate results, does it make any difference which one is used? Yes. It is a question of how sensitive

you want the alarm to be that will alert you to a developing trend. A very sensitive alarm is not without its costs.
Over this first time period the actual level of sales does
fluctuate quite a bit. Presumably, inventories are used to
smooth out the production on a month-to-month basis.
Over this time period both values for the error correction
factor do generate forecasts that average out to the average actual monthly figure of 444. So inventories would
neither build-up nor be depleted. The difference you do
get from the different error correction factors is in the
monthly fluctuations of the forecasts. With an error correction factor of .80, every time sales jump, production is
increased by 80% of the last error, just in case the increase
might be the beginning of a trend or a cyclical turning
point. If it is not a new trend or turning point, production
must be cut dramatically in the next time period. On the
other hand, with an error correction factor of only .20, we
believe that "one robin doesn't mean that spring is here."
We would take four time periods to get an 80% adjustment up.

However, when the upward trend develops in the last
25 periods on the graph, obviously the error adjustment
factor of .80 (the △s) does give much better results than
the forecasts generated by the error adjustment factor of
.20 (the 0s). The smaller error correction factor results in
production always lagging behind sales.

Forecasting techniques cannot remove the need for
business judgment. In a case like this the question is: How
much will it cost me to respond to short-term movements
that are just blips versus how much will it cost me to be
late in recognizing an emerging trend or turning point in

the cycle? That is a judgment call that can only be made with much more information than we have here, including such things as the cost of carrying excess inventory versus the cost of late deliveries.

VI.

The Use and Abuse
of Moving Averages

A *MOVING AVERAGE* IS AN average that moves along through a time series picking up a new data point and dropping an old one each time period. The first data point in a three-month moving average of a monthly time series would be the average of the first three months, for example, January, February and March. Usually this is plotted as a March data point. The next data point would be the average of February, March and April. For this second data point, plotted as April, we have dropped January and added April. In terms of the pressure curves we mentioned in Chapter IV, a 3/1 pressure curve would be the ratio of this month's three-month moving average to last month's.

There are two types of moving averages: *weighted and unweighted*. An unweighted moving average is really an equally weighted moving average. You would add January, February and March and divide the total by three. But suppose you felt that the world was changing so fast that more recent data should be given more weight.

In that case you might add up one January, plus two times February and three times March. Of course to get a monthly figure you would have to divide by six, not three. The weighting would be 1/6th to January, 2/6ths to February, and 3/6ths to March. In percentage terms the weights would be: 17% to January; 33% to February; and 50% to March. A weighted moving average simply gives more weight to more recent data while an unweighted moving average gives equal weight to all the data points included in the average.

Moving averages are used for three purposes: (1) as a specific numerical forecast for the next time period, (2) as a way to seasonally adjust a time series and (3) as a means to smooth our random movements so that the stage of the cycle is more apparent. Let us consider each in turn.

Exponential Smoothing as a Moving Average

In the last chapter we discussed exponential smoothing as a process of error correction. Another way to look at exponential smoothing is as a weighted moving average. What are the weights? We illustrated in the previous chapter that with an error correction factor of 100%, exponential smoothing merely amounts to a naive forecast of "next month to be the same level as this month." In other words, the most recent data point is given 100% weighting and all other data points are given zero. At the other extreme, with a 0% correction factor, the forecast would never be revised. The first (and oldest) data point would be given 100% weighting and all other (more recent) data would be given zero. So what we are interested in is the weighting when the error correction factor is larger than zero but less than 100%.

By mathematical exercises that we need not go into here, it can be shown that using exponential smoothing is the equivalent of forecasting using a moving average with weights that decline as the data get older. The weighting is highly sensitive to the size of the error correction factor. The following table illustrates the weighting that exponential smoothing gives to the most recent four data points with error correction factors of 20%, 50% and 80%:

Time Period	Error Correction Factor		
	20%	50%	80%
One previous	20%	50%	80%
Two previous	16%	25%	16%
Three previous	13%	12%	3%
Four previous	10%	6%	1%
Total most recent four periods	59%	93%	100%

The first thing to note is that the most recent data point, "one previous," gets the most weight. It receives a weight equal to the size of the error correction factor. All the other data points get the remaining portion of the 100% with declining weights as we go back in time. Even with an error correction factor of 20%, 59% of the total weighting is assigned to the most recent four periods. The older data points receive a total weighting of only 41%

By way of summary, a moving average of past data points can be used as a system to generate a specific forecast for the next data point. The error correction, or exponential smoothing, model is a system for doing this. It gives greater weights to the more recent data, and rapidly declining weights to the older data points. Specifically, an error correction model weights the most recent data point by a percentage equal to the error correction factor. The remainder of the percentage weighting is assigned to the older data at ever decreasing levels.

Seasonal and Trend Forecasting with a Moving Average

This author prefers the seasonal adjustment procedures presented in Chapter II. However, using a moving average to seasonally adjust data is a very common procedure. Indeed, virtually all the U.S. Government statistics that are seasonally adjusted are adjusted with a procedure based on moving averages.

Let us examine how a moving average of one year removes seasonal fluctuations. In the interest of keeping our computations short we'll use quarterly data. The following two years of data have only seasonal movement; there is no trend, cycle or random movement.

Year	Quarter	Data	Moving Total	Moving Average
1	1st	1		
1	2nd	2		
1	3rd	3		
1	4th	4	10	2.5
2	1st	1	10	2.5
2	2nd	2	10	2.5
2	3rd	3	10	2.5
2	4th	4	10	2.5

The sum of the four quarters is always 10, $1 + 2 + 3 + 4 = 10$; $2 + 3 + 4 + 1 = 10$; and so on. With the moving total unchanging at 10, the moving average is always 2.5, 10 divided by 4. So if all one has to deal with is seasonal fluctuations, a year-long moving average will give you a nice seasonally adjusted time series. You should be so lucky.

Let's complicate things a bit by using an example in which the actual time series is made up of a seasonal movement and a trend.

Year	Qtr.	(1) Seasonal	(2) Trend	(3) Data	(4) Moving Total	(5) Moving Average
1	1st	1	1	2		
1	2nd	2	2	4		
1	3rd	3	3	6		
1	4th	4	4	8	20	5
2	1st	1	5	6	24	6
2	2nd	2	6	8	28	7
2	3rd	3	7	10	32	8
2	4th	4	8	12	36	9
3	1st			?		

This time series is such that the actual data is equal to the repetitive seasonal plus the trend that increases one unit per time period. Column (3) equals column (1) plus column (2). Column (3), the "data," is the actual number we see and is the number we are trying to forecast. If we take a four quarter moving total of the data, we get column (4). Dividing column (4) by four gives us the moving average, column (5). Column (5) is a seasonally adjusted time series made up of pure trend movements: 5, 6, 7, 8 and 9.

Let's assume our job is to forecast the 1st quarter of year 3. We can look at the moving average, column (5), and reasonably forecast the 1st quarter of year 3 to have a value of 10. If the average is 10, the moving total, column (4), has to be 40, $4 \times 10 = 40$. If the moving total is 40, we can calculate the data point we need to complete column (3) by subtracting the previous three data points from the moving total to get a value of 10, $40 - 12 - 10 - 8 = 40 - 30 = 10$. Our forecast for the 1st quarter of year 3 is 10! If this seasonal pattern and trend were to continue it would be an accurate forecast.

Another way to reach the same forecast is to think in terms of the combined effects of trend and seasonal from the 4th quarter of year 2 to the 1st quarter of year 3. The moving average, column (5), reveals a trend value of +1 per quarter. We can go back and "detrend" the data to obtain the seasonal pattern. We would do this by subtracting 1 from the first data point, 2 from the second, 3 from the third and so on. The detrended time series would show the seasonal pattern of 1, 2, 3, 4 and repeating. In terms of quarter-to-quarter changes, the seasonal is +1, +1, +1, −3. From the 4th quarter of year 2 to the first quarter of year 3 we would expect a change of +1 trend and −3 seasonal for a net effect of −2. Since the actual data was 12 for the 4th quarter of year 2, we would expect 10 for the 1st quarter of year 3, $12 - 2 = 10$. The same result we obtained above.

Using a Moving Average to Find the Cycle

Another use of the moving average is simply to smooth out random "noise" in a time series. If a time series bounces around a lot, it is hard to tell a turning point from a "blip." Sometimes the use of a moving average can help distinguish a turning point from a random movement. How long a moving average do we have to use? How many data points? Academics who study these cycles state it in terms of determining the "months for cyclical dominance," the MCD. With monthly data, it is a question of how many months it takes the cyclical movement to offset or "dominate" the random movements. For a series without much random movement this can be just a few months. For a series with a lot of random fluctuations, it can be over a year.

As an example, we have shown earlier that housing starts have a distinct cycle. We also know that even after seasonal adjustment the series still fluctuates quite a bit. Figure 6 shows the annualized, seasonally adjusted monthly housing starts from January 1986 through December 1995 plotted with a three-month moving average. The three-month moving average takes out some of the extreme fluctuations, but still follows the original series closely with all its misleading ups and downs. Figure 7 shows a nine-month moving average, which in terms of helping you forecast, can be both good news and bad news. The good news is that when the nine-month moving average turns, something is definitely happening to the underlying series. The bad news

47

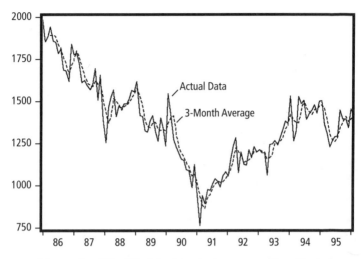

Figure 6.   Monthly housing starts, seasonally adjusted

Figure 7.   Monthly housing starts, seasonally adjusted

is that by the time you get the message, the turn has been under way for sometime.

The problem of what length of moving average to watch is very much like choosing the size of the error correction factor in exponential smoothing. If you choose a sensitive alarm (a three-month moving average), you get a lot of false alarms. If you choose a hard to convince indicator (a nine-month moving average), you will get the message well after the fact. This is another one of those tough business judgment calls. Of course, there is no law that says that you cannot watch both indicators. Many analysts do just that.

Moving Averages Can Be Dangerous

While moving averages are a good thing, on occasion analysts suffer from too much of a good thing. Running a moving average through a time series will always smooth it, but that is not always helpful to the analyst. What is noise to one analyst is useful information to another. If you were looking at retail sales and wanted to measure the impact of a big snowstorm in January, a twelve-month moving average would show that negative effect on the data plotted from January through the next December. Some analysts center their moving averages; that is, they plot the data on the month that is in the center. In the snowstorm example, the negative effect on retail sales would start showing up in June!

This analyst once conducted a study on the impact of interest rate changes on flows into various financial institutions. Other analysts found no impact. Of course, they were using data that had been seasonally adjusted by running moving averages through it. It had been smoothed to the extent that the impact of an interest rate change, which occurred on a particular business day, was lost. Simply using unadjusted data, or data adjusted in the manner described in Chapter II, made the impact of interest rates on financial flows apparent in the data.

If one gets too infatuated with moving averages—to the point of running moving averages of moving averages—one can really get into trouble. What happens is that cycles are generated where none existed before. Consider Figures 8 and 9. Figure 8 is a completely random series. The data plotted are computer generated random numbers, but they are plotted as if they were a time series. There is no cycle in this series. There is no trend. There is no seasonal to be removed. Figure 9 shows the result of

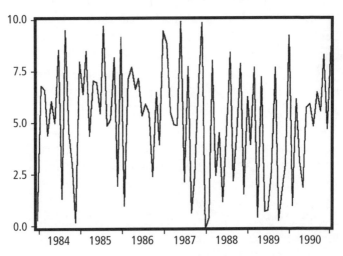

Figure 8. A random time series of 85 data points .

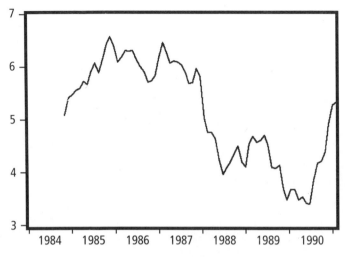

Figure 9.   A "12 x 2" moving average
of the random time series

running a twelve-point moving average and then taking the result and running a two-point moving average of that. A cycle appears—created by the analyst! It can be shown mathematically that, as you run moving averages, the result will get closer and closer to a perfectly symmetrical cycle. "Massaging" the data too much is always suspect. Or as the saying goes: "Torture your data enough, and it will confess!"

Beware when someone makes a presentation and says the data has been "filtered." That is techno-talk for running moving averages. Ask to see the raw, unfiltered data. If what you are looking for is not at least vaguely discernible in the raw data, be very skeptical about it being there at all. Remember, the raw data is the real world.

VII.

Using One Variable to Forecast Another

S O FAR WE HAVE only looked for patterns contained in the time series we are trying to forecast. Frequently, however, we suspect we can use knowledge of the influence of one time series on another. For example, it seems reasonable that a fall in temperature increases the consumption of heating oil. If our job is to make sure an apartment house does not run out of heating oil, we would be stupid to ignore the weather forecast. A way to quantify the relationship between temperature and heating oil consumption is to plot a scatter diagram with heating oil use on one axis and temperature on the other axis.

Consider the following illustration:

Day	Average of High and Low Temperature	Heating Oil Consumption
1	70	30
2	62	38
3	58	42
4	40	60
5	50	50

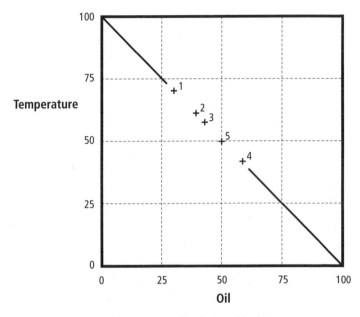

*Figure 10.   Idealized relationship between
temperature and oil consumption*

The scatter diagram of these data is shown in Figure 10. The number of the day indicates the spot that lines up with both the oil consumption and the temperature. Of course, we have rigged the data for illustrative purposes. We get a nice straight-line. Give me a temperature and I will tell you how much oil was burned. If a real cold snap were forecast, such that the temperature was expected to average 30 degrees, we would expect oil consumption to rise to 70. We might even determine this example is so simple that the two variables always add up to 100. If you want to know the heating oil consumption, just subtract the average temperature from 100. The world is rarely so simple!

The Real World, Employment and Output

Let us take some real world economic data and solve a more complicated forecasting problem. Table 12 contains eleven years of data on the unemployment rate for the U.S. economy. It also shows a naive forecast based on "next year, same as this year." Of course, such a naive forecast generates a set of error terms that are the same size, but opposite in sign, as the annual change in the unemployment rate. When the unemployment rate drops from 8.5 to 7.7 as it did from 1975 to 1976, the naive forecast of 8.5 for 1976 generates a positive error term equal to the .8 year-to-year change.

Year	% Unemp.	Naive Forecast	Error	% Chg. Real GDP
1975	8.5			-0.6
1976	7.7	8.5	0.8	5.6
1977	7.1	7.7	0.6	4.9
1978	6.1	7.1	1.0	5.0
1979	5.8	6.1	0.3	2.9
1980	7.2	5.8	-1.4	-0.3
1981	7.6	7.2	-0.4	2.5
1982	9.7	7.6	-2.1	-2.1
1983	9.6	9.7	0.1	4.0
1984	7.5	9.6	2.1	6.8
1985	7.2	7.5	0.3	3.7

Table 12. The unemployment rate and economic growth

The last column on the right in Table 12 is the rate of growth in the U.S. economy, "% Change in Real GDP." It is immediately obvious that the error terms and the % Change in Real GDP appear to move together. When economic growth is high, as it was in 1984 at 6.8, the unemployment rate falls from 9.6 to 7.5. This generates a large error of 2.1. Similarly, when GDP falls as in 1982, the unemployment rate rises from 7.6 to 9.7, giving us a large negative error term. If we can quantify this relationship, we can use the % Change in GDP to improve on the naive forecast of the unemployment rate.

To quantify the relationship between the error terms and the change in GDP, we plot the two time series on a scatter diagram, Figure 11. In Figure 11 the vertical axis (up and down) shows the % Change in GDP, while the horizontal axis shows the error term. To quantify this relationship precisely, we must "fit" a line through the points. There are many ways to do this. The line shown is just "eyeballed" in by the author. There are many computer programs that will fit a "least squares" line through the data points. If the fit is any good, the results from fitting the line one way or another will not vary that much. (When your staff say they have found a reliable relationship, ask to see the scatter diagram.)

In this case, the relationship seems to be a fairly good fit. So let's use it to improve our forecast of the unemployment rate. The sure way to get good results is to use it to forecast the years 1976–1985, because these are the years from which the relationship was derived. But, of course, if you already have 1976–1985, then you don't need to forecast those years! The honest way to test the relationship

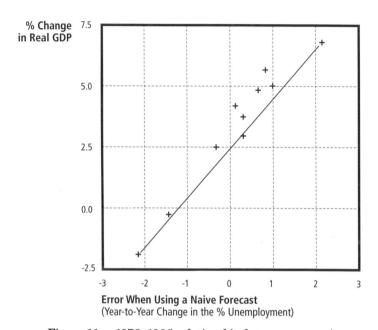

% Change in Real GDP

Error When Using a Naive Forecast
(Year-to-Year Change in the % Unemployment)

Figure 11. 1976–1985 relationship between economic growth and the change in the % unemployment

between two time series is to go "out of sample" for the test. In other words, we have found a relationship that appears to exist for the period 1976–1985; the real test is to determine if it will work in the future—for 1986–1995?

Table 13 shows the data for 1986–1995. In addition to the data columns shown in Table 12, Table 13 has three additional columns: an "adjustment factor," an "adjusted forecast" and another set of error terms. Where did those adjustment factors come from? From the straight-line drawn in by hand in Figure 7. For 1986, for example, the % Change in Real GDP is 3.0. Looking at Figure 11, we

	% Unemp.	Naive Forecast	Error	% Chg. Real GDP	Adjustment Factor	Adjusted Forecast	Error
1986	7.0	7.2	0.2	3.0	0.4	6.8	-0.2
1987	6.2	7.0	0.8	2.9	0.3	6.7	0.5
1988	5.5	6.2	0.7	3.8	0.6	5.6	0.1
1989	5.3	5.5	0.2	3.4	0.5	5.0	-0.3
1990	5.5	5.3	-0.2	1.3	-0.7	6.0	0.5
1991	6.7	5.5	-1.2	-1.0	-1.7	7.2	0.5
1992	7.4	6.7	-0.7	2.7	0.1	6.6	-0.8
1993	6.8	7.4	0.6	2.2	-0.1	7.5	0.7
1994	6.1	6.8	0.7	3.5	0.5	6.3	0.2
1995	5.6	6.1	0.5	2.0	-0.3	6.4	0.8
Sum of Absolute Errors			5.8				4.6
Average Absolute Error			0.6				0.5

*Table 13.   Forecasting the unemployment
rate using economic growth*

see that when we are on the vertical axis at 3.0 the
straight-line is over approximately .4 on the horizontal
axis. This implies that our naive forecast is likely to be
.4 too high. How can we improve it? By lowering it by
.4. Our naive forecast based on the previous year was 7.2.
We can correct it by subtracting the predicted error, .4, to
make our adjusted forecast 6.8. For 1986 the adjustment
does not reduce the absolute size of the error. It only
changes it from +.2 to −.2. However, for 1987 and 1988
the adjustment reduces the errors from .8 and .7, to .5
and .1. Overall, the adjustment reduces the sum of the
absolute errors from 5.8 to 4.6, over the ten years reduc-
ing the average absolute error from .6 to .5.

Samples for Testing and Samples for Forecasting

We have used a relationship estimated on the basis of 1976–1985 data to improve our forecasts for 1986–1985. This is the honest way to evaluate a forecasting technique, but it is not the only way. If our job were to forecast 1996, it would be foolish not to use the most recent data available. If we have the 1986–1995 data, we don't want to ignore it in forecasting 1996. In fact, we might want to give it more weight than the 1976–1985 data. The economy does change through time. More recent data may be a more reliable guide to the future than older data.

We have now complicated things enough so we have three choices for drawing our line through a scatter diagram. To obtain a 1996 adjustment in the unemployment rate to take account of the rate of economic growth: (1) we could use 1976–1985 data as we have just done, (2) we could use 1986–1995 data, or (3) we could combine the two and use 1976–1995. Actually, only (2) and (3) are worth considering. Why use only data that is a decade old?

Figure 12 is a scatter diagram using all 20 years, 1976–1995. The line fitted to these data is what I would use for a forecast for 1996. If real GDP is expected to grow by 2.5% in 1996, I would (by looking at the fitted line) estimate a correction factor of .2%. The average unemployment for 1995 generates a naive forecast of 5.6% for 1996. We correct that by .2% to get a forecast for 1996 of 5.4%.

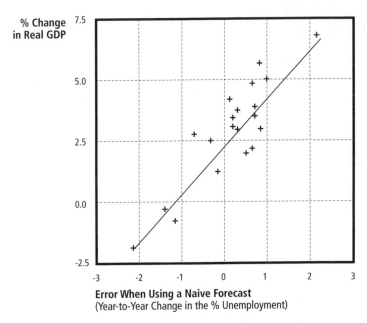

Figure 12. 1976–1995 relationship between economic growth and the change in the % unemployment

To conclude, it is wise to divide your data into different samples when looking for, and evaluating, a relationship between two variables. However, when it is time to forecast the future, it is wise to use everything you have. Base your forecast on either all the history available or on a subset of the most recent time periods. The world changes, so if you are going to drop anything, drop the old data.

VIII.

Bowers's Rules for Successful Forecasting

#1
If You Must Forecast, Forecast Frequently

Forecasting is not something you do once a year. Decisions are made every day, so forecasts must be made every day. We must continuously observe the difference between our earlier forecasts and what actually happens. New information is always being made available. We learn. We adjust. In many cases, all we can expect of a good forecast is for it to steer us in the right direction. We have to count on continuous monitoring and appropriate midcourse corrections to keep us on track.

How often should you forecast? As often as new data becomes available.

#2
Don't Judge a Long-Term Forecast by Its Accuracy

As you may have observed from your TV weatherman, the further out in time one forecasts, the less accurate the forecast is likely to be. Most TV weathermen only report on the prospects for the next five days and leave the long-term prospects to the *Farmer's Almanac.* As a general rule, we lower our expectations of accuracy considerably when the forecast is for the long-term.

In business planning, forecasts of five years or longer are notoriously inaccurate. Rarely does a business organization, large or small, bother to go back and compare current results to what was predicted five years earlier. Then why does anyone bother with five-year plans? Because the *process* of developing an internally consistent five-year plan can raise many important questions. Something as simple as the statement that "If we grow at 7-1/2% for the next five years, we will be 44% larger than we are today," can bring forth very useful contingency planning. Even if the truth turns out to be that the total growth over the next five years is as low as 30%, or as high as 50%; the forecast can have had a positive impact on the organization.

The fact is that most of the benefit of five-year plans comes from the process of developing the plan. The meetings and communications that are required to develop a five-year plan are generally very beneficial to the organization. The actual plan that results from all this activity will turn out to bear only the vaguest similarity to what actually happens. I often say to corporate planners that although it is important to go through all the anguish of developing a five-year plan, when it is complete you can throw it away! It is the process of creating the plan that yields the benefits, not the numbers that result from it.

Of course, long-term forecasts must always be supplemented by short-term forecasts. See rule #1, above.

#3
Always Be on the Lookout for Negative Feedback

By negative feedback, we mean that a jump in sales this month implies a fall in sales next month. I once developed a sales forecasting model for a manufacturing company which had highly variable month-to-month sales. Part of the reason for the high variability was that the company periodically held sales contests with substantial prizes for the salespeople and the customers—all-expense-paid cruises to exotic vacation spots. In the month when the contest closed sales went through the roof. Of course, the next month sales dropped dramatically. Upon closer examination, I found this up and down pattern to be true not just of contest periods. Each time a month was well above average, it would be followed by a month well below average. Why? The product was used in commercial construction. The company's various sales promotion tools neither caused any additional buildings to be built nor took market shares from competitors. It only served to shift sales from one month to another.

A good rule is: If this month's data is hard to believe, it is likely that next month's will be too—but in the opposite direction!

#4
Expect Forecasts to be Biased—
And Sometimes They Should Be

In Chapter I, we briefly mentioned a *biased* forecast. A biased forecast is one which tends, on average, to be consistently too high or too low. In various places in this book we have noted that in forecasting, analysts frequently have to make "judgment calls." Psychologists will tell us that our judgment is biased by our hopes, dreams and desires. So one needs to consider the possible bias of the person making the forecasts. If sales quotas are set on the basis of the sales forecasts, and if salespeople are rewarded for exceeding quota, one would expect a downward bias in a forecast generated by the sales force. On the other hand, senior management, seeking to motivate, would likely have an upward bias. When evaluating a forecast, both before and after the fact, *consider the source!*

Trying to motivate people or maximize one's own income may or may not be a good reason to deliberately bias a forecast in one direction or the other. However, there is one circumstance when it is scientifically valid to bias a forecast: when it costs substantially more to be wrong in one direction than it costs to be wrong in the other direction.

Consider the problem of forecasting financial flows for the purpose of cash management. If one overstates the need for readily available cash, the penalty is some lost interest income because money sits idle in a checking account when it could have been invested elsewhere—or used to pay off debt. The cost of forecasting high is lost interest income or additional interest cost. What is the cost of forecasting low? If you underestimate your need for readily available cash, you simply won't have money to pay your bills when due. No checks are sent out, or if checks are sent out, they bounce! The results can be disastrous. Suppliers cut you off, or worse yet, you are in bankruptcy court with a judge and your creditors having a considerable say in how you run your business. Given the difference in the penalties for being too high or too low—lost interest versus bankruptcy—I would feel comfortable with a built-in positive bias in a cash needs forecast. In fact, I would demand it.

#5
While Forecasting Is an Art, Not a Science, It Still Requires Hard Work

I want to conclude with a congratulations to the reader! If you have made it to this point in the book, you already know rule #5. Serious forecasting is hard work. Forecasting may be as much art as science, but woe be to the analyst who is not careful with numbers. The one thing that can totally remove any usefulness of a forecast, before anyone knows how accurate it is, is an arithmetic mistake. Many a presentation has gone down in flames when someone in the audience pointed out that the numbers were not the latest available, or worse yet, were simply wrong. It may not be fair, but one bad number throws a whole forecast into doubt. Always do those computations twice.

So may you be both lucky and smart, and may all your error terms be small ones.

FURTHER READING

Bails, Dale G., and Larry C. Peppers, *Business Fluctuations, Forecasting Techniques and Applications,* Second Edition. Englewood Cliffs, New Jersey: Prentice Hall, 1993.

Hanke, John E., and Arthur G. Reitsch, *Business Forecasting,* Third Edition. Boston: Allyn and Bacon, 1989.

Niemira, Michael P., and Philip A. Klein, *Forecasting Financial and Economic Cycles,* New York: John Wiley & Sons, Inc., 1994.

Newbold, Paul, and Theodore Bos, *Introductory Business & Economic Forecasting,* Second Edition. Cincinnati, Ohio: South-Western Publishing Co., 1994.

Pindyck, Robert S., and Daniel L. Rubinfeld, *Econometric Models & Economic Forecasts,* Third Edition. New York: McGraw-Hill, Inc., 1991.

ABOUT THE AUTHOR

Professor David A. Bowers is Chairman of the Department of Banking and Finance at the Weatherhead School of Management, Case Western Reserve University, where he teaches courses in banking, business cycles and economic forecasting. At Case Western Reserve University, he has also served as Chairman of the Department of Economics, and previously as Associate Dean for Professional Programs.

Professor Bowers has published two textbooks and numerous journal articles in such publications as the *Journal of the American Statistical Association,* the *Journal of Finance* and the *Journal of Political Economy.* His major research interests are in the areas of business cycles, interest rates and money markets.

Professional employment for Professor Bowers has ranged from Economist for a New York savings bank to Operations Research Engineer for an aircraft corporation. In addition to Case Western Reserve University, he has also held teaching appointments at New York University, Rice University and the University of Vermont.

Professor Bowers was born in Alice, Texas, and received his degrees from Texas A & M (bachelor's), Tulane University (master's) and Southern Methodist University (doctorate). He served on the Board of Directors of a local savings and loan association, and is Consultant and Speaker to numerous local and national financial and non-financial corporations.

Dr. David A. Bowers, Weatherhead School of Management, Case Western Reserve University, 10900 Euclid Avenue, Cleveland, Ohio 44106–7235